THOR: SON OF ASGARD
THE WARRIORS TEEN

AKIRA YOS

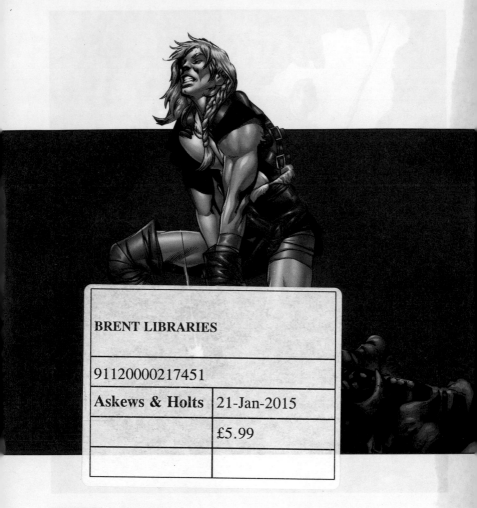

MARVEL *POCKET BOOK* Thor: Son Of Asgard - The Warriors Teen

Thor: Son Of Asgard - The Warriors Teen. Marvel Pocketbook Vol. 1. Contains material originally published in magazine form as Thor: Son of Asgard #1-6 & Jounrey Into Mystery #97-103. First printing 2011. Published by Panini Publishing, a division of Panini UK Limited. Mike Riddell, Managing Director. Alan O'Keefe, Managing Editor. Mark Irvine, Production Manager. Marco M. Lupoi, Publishing Director Europe. Ed Hammond, Reprint Editor. Charlotte Reilly, Designer. Office of publication: Brockbourne House, 77 Mount Ephraim, Tunbridge Wells, Kent TN4 8BS. MARVEL, X-Men and all related characters and the distinctive likenesses thereof: TM & © 1964, 2004 & 2011 Marvel Entertainment, LLC and its subsidiaries. Licensed by Marvel Characters B.V. No similarity between any of the names, characters, persons and/or institutions in this edition with those of any living or dead person or institution is intended, and any such similarity which may exist is purely coincidental. This publication may not be sold, except by authorised dealers, and is sold subject to the condition that it shall not be sold or distributed with any part of its cover or markings removed, nor in a mutilated condition. This publication is produced under licence from Marvel Characters B.V. through Panini S.p.A. Printed in Italy. www.marvel.com. All rights reserved. ISBN: 978-1-84653-139-2

THOR: SON OF ASGARD

THOR: SON OF ASGARD
THE WARRIORS TEEN

CONTENTS

Asgard. Home of the mighty Norse gods...

"To enter the Kingdom of Asgard is no easy task. We must first cross Bifrost, the mystic Rainbow Bridge, the sole entrance to the eternal city and its surrounding lands.

"We may only cross the shimmering expanse into Asgard if given pass by the ever-vigilant Heimdall, guardian of the Bridge."

The Square of the All-Father.

"The central gathering place for the denizens of Asgard, used for occasions and events of all kinds; for the gathering of troops before war; for celebrations in times of victory; for the issuance of imperial decrees.

"Designed to win respect and establish absolute authority, the revered square is a place of power, which is, not surprisingly, located directly at the foot of..."

The Imperial Palace of Asgard!

"After crossing the threshold through the main entrance of the palace, we emerge in the Great Hall of Heroes. Lined with memorials to warriors who have given their lives in blind service to Asgard, this Hall leads to the ultimate seat of power.

"Behind the Doors of Dramir lies the throne room of...

"Odin, the All-Father, King of all Asgard!"

"From his majestic throne, Odin rules Asgard and the lands beyond with the wisdom, cunning and compassion he has learned over countless years."

"A cabinet of trusted advisors aid him in governing the day-to-day affairs of the kingdom..."

"...and a contingent of savvy warriors help him keep the peace and protect his lands from outside threats."

"Odin's rule extends far and wide across the Nine Worlds. His attention is often required on many matters and in many places at the same time.

"But, there are some things that, occasionally, manage to escape the gaze of even the most omniscient ruler..."

The WARRIORS TEEN Part 1

AKIRA YOSHIDA
WRITER

GREG TOCCHINI
PENCILER

JAY LEISTEN
INKER

GURU eFX
COLORIST

ADI GRANOV
COVER ARTIST

VIRTUAL CALLIGRAPHY'S
RANDY GENTILE
LETTERER

MACKENZIE CADENHEAD
EDITOR

RALPH MACCHIO & C.B. CEBULSKI
CONSULTING EDITORS

JOE QUESADA
EDITOR IN CHIEF

DAN BUCKLEY
PUBLISHER

While I appreciate your support, Sif, I know that nothing is set in stone.

Though I'm the son of a ruler, that doesn't automatically make me fit to rule.

No matter how hard I try to prove myself.

And there is no need for modesty here, Balder. It's you who are beloved across Asgard, by all creatures large and small.

You're a natural warrior with skills that surpass even my own.

Mjolnir belongs in *your* hands.

As Odin is so quick to remind us, "Whosoever holds this hammer, if he be worthy..."

If anyone's worthy of wielding the mystic weapon at this time, it's you, Balder.

Thor, I don't--

Don't worry, I said, "...at this time..."

Who knows what will happen in the future?

I'll be worthy someday, I know I will. And then I'll come to claim the hammer as my own!

But Father, Loki--

No, Thor, you will not question my decision on this. Just as you three have your paths in life, Loki has his. And those paths are not meant to cross just yet.

Excuse me, Lord Odin. Where will this new path that Thor has set us upon take the three of us?

The time has come to forge a new enchanted weapon. A sword this time. A sword, which once cast, I will bestow upon the Asgardian warrior most deserving of it.

However, I have need of four mystic elements that I will use in the sword's creation. Four elements that you three will travel Asgard to collect for me.

"First, you will make your way to Nastrond, where dragons still dwell. There you will retrieve a single scale from the hide of the dragon Hakurei, which, when forged in the sword, will make its blade unbreakable.

"From there, you will travel to the snowy peaks of Jotunheim, where you will pluck a feather from the wing of the snow eagle Gnori. This will help make the sword light in hand and swift in motion.

"Then, you will continue on to Jennia, where you must unearth a jewel from deep in the mines there... a jewel, which, when placed in the hilt, will maintain the sword's balance.

"Lastly, you will journey to Lilitha, where you will draw a small vial of water from the Lake of Lilitha... enchanted water that will ensure the sword remains ever pure."

These are the tasks I set before you on this quest. Is there anything further you would ask of me?

Nothing? Excellent.

I suggest you head to your rooms and begin preparation. You leave at dawn.

"And so, the next morning, the son of Odin and his two friends begin their journey into the wilds of Asgard. While they leave the safety of the castle behind them, Odin will no doubt keep a close eye on their adventures."

"But there are some things that, occasionally, manage to escape the gaze of even the most omniscient ruler...

"Things with a purpose different from those of a loving father...

"Evil things...

"Reaching for those we often hold dearest in our hearts."

Enough with the silent treatment!

We're friends. We speak our minds. Let's clear the air here.

The daggers your eyes have silently been shooting into my back are starting to take their toll.

You're right, Thor. We are friends. But friends usually like to be asked their opinions before being dragged into situations they may not particularly care for.

What are you saying, Balder? You didn't want to come on this quest? You would have preferred to hide at home rather than join the adventure Odin has set us on?

I believe what Balder is getting at is that we would have appreciated having some say in the matter. Our lives are our own. The choice should have been ours.

You know Sif and I would follow you through the Gates of Hel, Thor. But we would prefer to do it of our own free will.

You jumped at the chance to go on this quest just to please your father. You never once asked us if we wanted to come along with you. You just assumed we would.

You, my two closest friends, would *refuse* the chance to be part of this grand journey? Even when asked by Odin?

That's just the point, Thor! We were never asked! We weren't even given the chance to refuse!

This isn't about courage or pride. It's about respect-- the respect one friend has for another to **ask** for her help rather than simply assume it.

Of all the sons of Asgard, I would never have expected this of you, Balder. A true warrior would never refuse a challenge set forth by Lord Odin.

And what of this daughter of Asgard?! Does the fact that I'm female make me any less a warrior than either of you?! You think I'm just some girl, unfit for such a masculine escapade?!

You think I'm here to simply tag along as you two fight the battles and claim Odin's prizes?!

LOOKING
FOR ME?

HA
HAHAHA
HAHA

THEY
DIDN'T TELL YOU I
COULD SPEAK, DID
THEY?

WELL, I
GUESS *THESE* ARE THE
LAST WORDS YOU WILL
EVER HEAR.

FWWWHSSSH

This is not at all what I expected.

He was waiting for us. He knew we were coming.

It doesn't really matter **why** he's here. The fact of the matter is that the dragon Hakurei **is** here.

Odin asked us to collect a scale from his impenetrable hide... and that's what we're going to do.

His presence here only makes our task that much easier.

Thor, wait!

RRAARRGGHH!

And don't forget about me, beast!

Thor!

FWAASH

Thor's almost reached his perch.

Come on, Sif, we have to lure Hakurei that way.

Spirits of the Vanna, grant me your wings.

You did it, Thor! That's the way to strike a blow!

You brought down the dragon!

No. I didn't win this fight alone. Victory is *ours!*

Your strategy was sound, Balder. I should have consulted with you before rushing into battle.

But next time you can run, while I distract the dragon.

I hope you didn't think I was running scared, Sif. Never doubt my integrity and skills as a warrior and I'll never insult yours again.

You've proven yourself our equal more times than I can count. If you hadn't held your own against Hakurei today, we might not be standing here victorious.

Can you both forgive me for my earlier attitude and actions? I was a fool and only suceeded in driving us apart. Let this victory bring harmony back to the group again.

Let's unite our swords as a symbol of our unbreakable bond.

For Asgard!

What kind of mad quest has Odin sent us on? From fire to ice! We've traveled from one extreme to the other.

A mad quest Odin sent us on or a mad quest *you accepted?*

Just whose fault is it that we're up here freezing to death?

I've heard about enough out of you, Balder. I've apologized for agreeing to this quest without asking you first. I've admitted I was wrong.

Can *you* not accept that? What more do you want from me?!

A fire and a warm meal would be nice...

Enough!

UUGHH!!

FUMF

Leave him alone, Thor!

Just as Sif has figured out their attack, I think I may have figured out their weakness.

These ice pixies are some form of elemental. They must remain in constant contact with the substance they are drawing their power from.

In this case, they're channeling the ice that lies beneath the snow we're standing on. They can keep reforming while touching it. Break their connection to that ice and they become powerless.

THUMP

KRSSH

PWOHF

Just like with the dragon, it's as if someone knew we were coming.

Someone who wants to prevent us from accomplishing our tasks.

Someone who wants us dead, more likely!

I don't care what you think, Thor, but this is no coincidence. Someone knows about our quest!

And again I'll remind you that no one but Odin knows of this journey we're on.

Loki was there. He was asked to leave but could have overheard...

You're always so quick to blame my brother, Sif! Loki would never--

SCREEEEEE

SCREEEEEE

Just what do you speak of, King Gnori? Balder is the most noble and gentle of souls in all these lands.

How can love spell doom for one such as he, against whom none can bear ill will?

Your senses are keen, Lady Sif, much like those of your brother, Heimdall. But there is still much that passes you by.

There is no destiny that is set in stone. No future that cannot be changed. You must learn to see all the possibilities presented for what they truly are and choose your path wisely.

King Gnori, I beg your forgiveness. My earlier accusations were spoken in haste and anger. I meant no disrespect. My harsh words only serve to bring shame to my name and that of my family. Please find it in your heart to forgive me.

You may rise, Odinson.

There is no need for such apologies, Thor. While you were quick to place blame, your words came from your heart and were spoken out of concern for the lives of your friends. I would expect no less.

You are indeed your father's son.

And if I am not mistaken, your father has requested you bring him one of these?

Please take one. You have all earned it.

Fare thee well, young gods. I expect great things from you!

HELP!

SIF?!

Fear not, Sif, I'm--

Thor! Sif! I heard the sounds of a struggle. Are you--??

"Fairly certain Balder will stay away until you call for him", eh?

HAHAHA   HAHAHA

What happened? Why are you two lying there like that?

Have I missed something here?

The evil eye?

Just what did you do, Thor?

Oh, yes, Balder. You missed quite the show--

Unbelievable! Is there nothing I can do to weaken the bonds of friendship these three share?

The next afternoon...

Once we reach the end of the forest, we should find ourselves at the Dunes of Jennia.

And we have to cross the dunes to reach the mines?

There's no other way.

Don't worry. Maybe we can find another pool later where you can wash the sand off.

That's enough of that, Thor.

SWAK

Well, I guess this is where I now become Sif the Sandy.

Enough of what? Care to share, my friends?

Oh, it's nothing, Balder.

Really? Why not tell me and let me be the judge of that?

Don't mind him, Balder, Thor needs to learn to keep his mouth shut.

Let's just keep going...

Fine! Keep your secrets to yourselves.

Look! See there in the distance? That must be the entrance to the Mines of Jennia. It's not so far after all.

Good. Let's take a quick break and then be on our way.

This might be the first time neither of you has complained about a task on this quest.

≈sigh≈

The day is still young, Thor...

Thor and Sif, both swallowed by these sands. But why? And to what end?

Could they survive? If so, where are they? And what are they doing...

...alone *together*?

Your powers of observation are the best in all Asgard, Balder. You were able to figure out the truth about the Jennia from simply watching us vanish?

It wasn't so much your disappearing as it was remembering what you said and did just before you were swallowed.

Gif expressed desire for a jewel of her own. And your anger ran unchecked after she was swallowed, Thor. Desire and anger are two of the strongest emotions we know.

Thinking back, I remember hearing rumors of the jewels' power as a child.

They said "To possess too many..."

"...is to lose much more." I also remembered the stories. And it all added up.

It was emotion that they spoke of losing, as the jewels would suck it from you.

And it must be for that reason that Odin needs a Jennia jewel!

He said he needed the jewel to provide balance to the sword he wishes to forge.

But not to simply balance the blade... to also balance the bearer!

And the Jennia who attacked us fed on our emotions in order to protect their jewels?

In a manner of speaking, yes. But the Jennia **are** the jewels. Or at least, become them...

I think that the jewels are actually the hardened hearts of Jennia who have passed on. Their now emotionless souls are captured in the jewels.

Now it's off to Lilitha for the last of Odin's elements.

Thank you, Balder.

SMOOCH

You used your mind to triumph where our muscle could not. A trait of a true warrior.

What emotion do you think is the most powerful? Love?

Possibly. But let's not forget love's opposite.

Hatred is an equally strong emotion.

Too true, Thor. Anyone who enters these sands with hate in their heart is surely doomed to a fate most unkind.

I speak the truth. Karnilla intends to take Asgard as her own. Believe me... please.

WUMP

Tell me why, Loki?

Why come to us with this news now when you have shown us nothing but contempt in the past?

Yes, it is true there is no love lost between us. I'll admit that.

However, any hatred I feel for you three is outweighed by my love for my father, Odin.

A father who took me in.

A father who gave me a chance at life.

A father whose own life is now in danger.

A father who needs our help.

The Lake of Lilitha...

It's gone!

What magic is this?! How could--

Karnilla!

NNOOOOO!!!!

You will pay dearly for this, witch!

But I will not leave these lands empty-handed. I will bring a token of the lake as a reminder of my failure today so I will never taste such bitterness again.

To Asgard.

This is not exactly the homecoming I had envisioned, Father.

THOR: SON
OF ASGARD
#6 COVER

Victory in battle may have escaped me this day...

...but by taking the life of their beloved prince, I have struck a blow against Asgard that shall never be forgotten!

Odin is sure to seek quick retribution.

I shall take advantage of this confusion, finish here and be quickly gone.

What business could the Queen of Norn possibly have in the chambers of the King of Asgard?!

CHUD

None walk away from Mjolnir's blow when dealt by the hand of Odin.

Now, Karnilla, it is time--

No.

Thor...

Forgive me, Thor. By sending you on this quest, I also sent you to your death.

I hoped to see my son become a man.

I hoped to see my son become King.

I hoped to see my son rule Asgard.

But now all I will see is my son buried too young.

My Lord, there are no words to describe the breaking of a heart... but ours have been shattered by the tragedy this day.

Asgard will mourn Thor's passing. He was beloved by all.

Most of all by you both.

A father's love for his son is expected... often taken for granted.

A friend's love, however, must be earned and given freely.

Balder, since you were children, you have stood by Thor's side, supporting and protecting him. Never once did your loyalty to your friend falter.

Although your blood does not flow through my veins, Thor was like a brother to me.

And Sif, Thor's life would have been empty if not for your kindness and compassion. You lightened his heart and helped ease his burdens.

It was Thor who often brightened our days and brought joy to our lives. Never has there been a soul more kind and more noble than your son, my Lord.

Bless you, milady.

I lost my son... but you lost a friend.

The pain and suffering shall be ours to bear...

...but ours to share.

Farewell....

What in Hela's name...?!

SPLOCH

What happened here?

Bless the branches of Yggdrasill! THOR LIVES!!

Please, Father, tell me what happened. Why does all of Asgard stare at me?

You fell in battle, my son. Not moments ago, you lay dead before our eyes in this very spot.

But how is this possible? The arrow left no mark...

We owe your life to the power of love and the Lake of Lilitha.

In my grief, I scattered the dried lake bed dirt over your body, knowing that we could draw water from it to save your life if touched by love's tears.

However, omniscience does not grant me the ability to control fate. I could only set the stage and hope that events would take their natural course. When Sif's tears came into contact with the enchanted earth, their healing powers brought you back to life.

LOKI!

Oh, come now. Secretly, you wish this young trickster dead, do you not? After all the trouble he's caused, would your lives not be easier without him?

From alerting the dragon to conjuring the rock troll, it was Loki here who tried to sabotage your ridiculous quest at every turn. He would rather see *you* all dead.

Please.... no....

While all you say may be true, Karnilla, in the end, Loki chose the path of righteousness.

By warning us of your impending attack, it was Loki who raised the alarm and saved all of Asgard.

Are those the actions of someone who would want us all dead?

I think not.

How can you defend him? His hands are as dirty as mine.

My hands... that will spill blood once more today.

If you must take a life this day... take mine.

I forfeit it in exchange for Loki's.

And if the denizens of Asgard hate Loki, as you say, won't my death better satisfy your need for revenge?

Balder, are you alright? What just happened?

The Norn Queen-- Where has she gone?

Fear not, my friends. I have a feeling we will not be seeing Karnilla again anytime soon.

What do you mean? She could still be lurking in the shadows...

No, Lady Sif, she will not be back this day.

Balder has opened her eyes to something she never knew existed. Something that will keep her occupied for quite some time.

Today was a day every father fears... a day in which I almost lost both my sons.

It is a day I hope I will never be forced to live again.

I am thankful beyond belief that you escaped with your lives.

But there are some who were not as lucky...

Citizens of Asgard, the victory that is ours this day comes at a heavy cost. The lives of many Asgardians have been lost in defense of our land. We must ensure their sacrifices were not made in vain. We will restore Asgard to the glory it once knew!

Amidst today's darkness we can also find a light of hope, for Asgard welcomes these new warriors into our ranks. Without their courage and fortitude, the battle may not have been won.

Tomorrow Agnar and Gotron will journey to meet Sindri, the King of the Dwarves. They will present him with four mystic elements that he will forge into a sword.

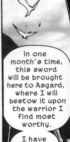

In one month's time, this sword will be brought here to Asgard, where I will bestow it upon the warrior I find most worthy.

I have much to consider.

One month later. The Imperial Banquet Hall.

So, who do you think it's going to be? Upon whom will Odin bestow the sword?

It's not like we haven't talked about this every day for the last month, Sif.

All I can say is that I don't believe this sword is meant for me.

There's another enchanted weapon that belongs in my hands. When I am worthy...

Someday.

Tonight, let us remember our fallen comrades. Our brothers who gave their lives protecting Asgard. We honor these brave warriors as they join our forefathers in Valhalla.

Yet, while we have suffered losses that we shall mourn, there have been triumphs to recognize. These three young Asgardians have proven themselves worthy of our company.

The Lady Sif, with her keen senses and unswerving loyalty, joins the growing number of warrior maidens in our ranks.

Balder the Brave, whose sound strategies and respect for all life makes him a valuable addition to our number.

And my own son, Thor, whose vigor and valor rivals that of any warrior present, shall bring his passion into each and every battle we will fight.

I sent these three on a quest to obtain four mystic elements which have now been forged into the enchanted sword you see here.

Warriors of Asgard, I present to you...

Svadren!

This sword is one of the most powerful weapons seen anywhere in the Nine Worlds. It is a weapon of honor, of pride and of courage.

It is a weapon that I now bestow upon the Asgardian warrior whom I feel most deserves it...

TALES OF... **ASGARD!**

HOME OF THE MIGHTY NORSE **GODS**

BEFORE MAN COULD READ OR WRITE, HE HAD HIS LEGENDS! AND NO LEGENDS WERE MORE THRILLING, MORE COLORFUL, MORE FILLED WITH FANTASY AND HIGH ADVENTURE THAN THE LEGENDS OF **ASGARD**, HOME OF THE GODS! THUS, WITH GREAT PRIDE, WE PRESENT THIS NEW, TREND-SETTING SERIES, BASED UPON HIGHLIGHTS OF NORSE MYTHOLOGY-- TALES OF **ASGARD**, THE BIRTHPLACE OF THE MIGHTY **THOR**!!

WRITTEN BY:
STAN LEE
DRAWN BY:
JACK KIRBY

INKED BY
G. BEL

HEROIC LEGENDS CAN ONLY ORIGINATE FROM A HEROIC PEOPLE... AND NONE WERE MORE HEROIC THAN THE ANCIENT NORSEMEN WHO STRUGGLED VALIANTLY AGAINST WILD BEASTS AND WILDER WEATHER!

NO NORSEMAN COULD EVER RELAX HIS VIGIL! ALMOST DAILY, THE HARDY FARMERS AND THEIR WOMENFOLK WERE FORCED TO TAKE UP ARMS AGAINST SAVAGE RAIDERS FROM THE MOUNTAINS!

AND THOSE WHO TURNED TO THE SEA WERE THE MOST FEARLESS OF ALL! THEIR COURAGE AND DARING WILL LIVE ON AS LONG AS MEN TELL OF VALOR-- FOR WHO AMONG US HAS NOT THRILLED TO THE TALES OF THE ANCIENT VIKINGS??!

YES, SUCH ARE THE NORSEMEN... THE BRAVE, STOUT-HEARTED WARRIORS WHO CHANTED THE LEGENDS OF ASGARD AROUND THEIR CAMPFIRES -- WHO CREATED HEROES AND GODS AND DEMONS WHICH STILL FIRE THE IMAGINATION OF MEN!

2

TO THE NORSEMEN, THEIR LEGENDARY CHARACTERS WERE EITHER ALL *GOOD* OR ALL *BAD!* THEIR GOOD GODS WERE CALLED THE *ÆSIR*--AND THEY FOUGHT FOR AGES AGAINST THE TOTALLY EVIL *FRONT GIANTS!*

AND THE PLACE WHERE THEY DWELLED WAS BOUNDED BY THE LAND OF *FIRE* ON THE SOUTH, AND THE LAND OF *MIST* ON THE NORTH!

AT THE WORLD'S END SAT *SURTUR,* THE DEMON OF FIRE, WHO WAITED, WITH HIS FLAMING SWORD, FOR THE END OF THE WORLD, WHEN HE MIGHT GO FORTH TO DESTROY GODS AND MEN ALIKE!

AND BENEATH ALL LAY THE MAGICAL *WELL OF LIFE!* IT WAS FROM THIS WELL THAT ALL THE RIVERS FLOWED -- RIVERS WHICH WERE TURNED INTO HUGE BLOCKS OF ICE BY THE CRUEL, NORTHERN WINDS!

3

FINALLY, AFTER COUNTLESS CENTURIES, A STRANGE FORM OF **LIFE** MAGICALLY APPEARED! THE TONS OF ICE WHICH HAD BEEN FORMING ABOVE THE **WELL OF LIFE** CHANGED THEIR SHAPE, AND TURNED INTO **YMIR**, GREATEST OF ALL THE EVIL **FROST GIANTS!**

SECONDS LATER, **ANOTHER** FORM OF LIFE APPEARED -- THIS WAS A GIGANTIC MAGIC **COW**, WHOSE MILK PROVIDED NOURISHMENT FOR THE MONSTROUS **YMIR!** AND, FOR AGES, **YMIR** AND THE MAGIC COW ROAMED THE FROZEN WASTES, UNTIL...

...ONE DAY THE MAGIC COW FOUND SOMETHING STIRRING IN THE ICE! AT FIRST, IT WAS UNRECOGNIZABLE...

...BUT THEN, SLOWLY, POWERFULLY, A NOBLE **HEAD** APPEARED ABOVE THE ICE...

AND THUS THE FIRST OF THE GOOD **ÆSIR** CAME INTO BEING! LOOK WELL AT HIM! LOOK WELL AT THE ONE CALLED **BURI!** FOR THOSE WHO FOLLOW HIM SHALL BE **GODS!**

4

BURI GREW WISE, AND STRONG, AND ONE DAY TOOK HIM A WIFE! THEN HE HAD A SON NAMED BORR! AND YEARS LATER BORR WAS MARRIED AND HAD THREE SONS OF HIS OWN! BUT OH, WHAT SONS THEY WERE -- FOR ONE WAS NAMED -- ODIN!!!

ODIN!! CALLED THE ALL-FATHER! ODIN!! GREATEST OF ALL NORSE GODS! ODIN! SUPREME WARRIOR WHO SLAYED THE LAST OF THE ICE GIANTS, THUS BRINGING ABOUT THE FIRST TRIUMPH OF GOOD OVER EVIL!

ODIN, AND TWO BROTHERS SOON TURNED THEIR ATTENTION TO EARTH! FOR THERE WAS MUCH ABOUT EARTH THAT WAS BEAUTIFUL -- MUCH ABOUT EARTH THAT THEY LOVED! AND SO, THEY SET A RING AROUND THE PLANET, AND THE MAGIC TREE YGGDRASILL GREW UP AND SPREAD ITS BRANCHES OVER EARTH, AND PROTECTED IT WHILE AWAITING THE COMING OF MAN!

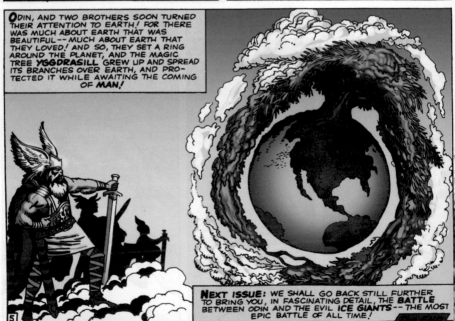

NEXT ISSUE: WE SHALL GO BACK STILL FURTHER TO BRING YOU, IN FASCINATING DETAIL, THE BATTLE BETWEEN ODIN AND THE EVIL ICE GIANTS -- THE MOST EPIC BATTLE OF ALL TIME!

THE END

IN HIS IMPERIAL CASTLE, ON THE HIGHEST PEAK OF THE TALLEST MOUNT IN ALL OF ASGARD, NOBLE *ODIN*, LORD OF THE GODS, HEARS THE CALL TO BATTLE!

THE TRUMPET BLARES! THE TIME HAS COME! I MUST DESTROY THE ICE GIANTS!

RIDING A GOLDEN CHARIOT, DRAWN BY HIS MAGNIFICENT WINGED STALLIONS, THE RULER OF ALL THE GODS THUNDERS THRU THE SKIES...

FASTER, MY MIGHTY MOUNTS! MY BLADE HUNGERS FOR COMBAT... MY SOUL THIRSTS FOR REVENGE!

BEHOLD! ODIN JOINS THE BATTLE!

WHEN *HE* IS SLAIN, ALL OF ASGARD SHALL BE OURS!

BUT, THOUGH DWARFED IN SIZE BY HIS GIGANTIC FOES, THE VALIANT ODIN DRAWS BACK HIS MAGIC SWORD AS HIS DEAFENING WAR CRY REVERBERATES THRU THE HEAVENS...

DEATH TO THE ENEMIES OF ASGARD!

2

SUMMONING THE AWESOME FORCES OF NATURE TO HIS BEHEST, THE MONARCH OF ASGARD HURLS MIGHTY *METEOR BOLTS* AT THE FEARSOME FRIGID BEHEMOTHS WHO ARE MENACING HIS DOMAIN.!

BUT, THOSE OF THE ICE GIANTS WHO SURVIVE MIGHTY BLASTS USE THEIR DEADLY ICE-CLUBS AGAINST ODIN, TRYING TO BATTER HIM FROM THE SKIES.!

UNABLE TO STRIKE THE SWIFTLY-DARTING CHARIOT, THEY THEN RESORT TO THEIR MOST POTENT POWER... IN UNISON, THE ICE GIANTS UNLEASH A TITANIC GUST OF FROZEN NORTH WIND, HURLING THEIR NOBLE FOE FROM HIS CRAZILY-SPINNING CHARIOT.!

AS THE GRACEFUL WINGED STALLIONS FLY OFF, ODIN LANDS ATOP THE MOUNTAIN ON WHICH THE ICE GIANTS STAND...

THEN, AS HIS CONFIDENT FOES CREEP SLOWLY TOWARDS HIM, MIGHTY ODIN DRAWS BACK HIS MAGIC SWORD...

3

...AND STRIKES, SPLITTING THE ENTIRE MOUNTAIN IN TWO, WITH ONE INCREDIBLE BLOW!

UNPREPARED FOR ODIN'S SUDDEN MANEUVER, THE CONFUSED TITANS FALL INTO THE NEWLY-FORMED CHASM, WHERE THE DEMONS OF SURTUR WAIT GREEDILY BELOW, TO MAKE THEM PRISONERS FOR ALL TIME!

DOWN, YOU MARAUDING MONSTERS! SO PLUNGE YOU TO SURTUR'S FIERY DOMAIN... WHERE YOU SHALL MENACE ASGARD NO MORE!

BUT ONE FROZEN BEHEMOTH STILL REMAINS! THIS, THE MIGHTIEST, THE MOST SAVAGE OF ALL, IS YMIR, KING OF THE ICE GIANTS!

VICTORY IS NOT YET YOURS, ACCURSED ODIN! MY ICY SPEAR SHALL YET BRING YOU TO YOUR KNEES!

HAH! I HAVE DISLODGED THE PEAK ON WHICH YOU HIDE LIKE A FEARFUL FLEA! AND NOW, I SHALL END YOUR REIGN FOREVER!

NOT SO, EVIL YMIR! WHILE BREATH REMAINS IN ME I SHALL FIGHT YOU! AND, BY MY BEARD, THE VICTORY SHALL YET BE MINE!

4

YOUR WORDS ARE BRAVE, BUT YOUR DEEDS MAKE A MOCKERY OF THEM! EVEN NOW, AS YOU RETREAT IN COWARDLY PANIC, I SHALL SEIZE YOU...AND DESTROY YOU!

BUT, REACHING THE ARRID, VOLCANIC AREA HE SEEKS, THE MONARCH OF THE GODS SUDDENLY STOPS, TURNS, AND THEN...

I HAVE TRAPPED YOU, YMIR! BEFORE YOU CAN MAKE ANOTHER MOVE, I STRIKE THIS VERY SPOT...

...RELEASING THE ONE FORCE WHICH CAN DEFEAT YOU... THE FIERY, SMOLDERING *FLAMES* FROM THE DEPTHS BELOW!

AND SO YMIR, THE LAST OF THE DREADED ICE GIANTS, BECOMES AN ETERNAL PRISONER ON THAT BARREN SPOT, SURROUNDED BY A WALL HE CAN NEVER PENETRATE!

WHILST NOBLE ODIN, RULER OF THE GODS, RETURNS TO HIS THRONE IN ASGARD!

THE END

NEXT ISSUE: SURTUR the FIRE DEMON

5

ODIN PRESSES ON, EVEN THOUGH THE TROLL KING THREATENS HIM WITH DEATH IF HE DOES NOT LEAVE THE FORBIDDEN LAND!

AND THEN, THE TROLLS ATTACK HEROIC ODIN! *ODIN*, WHOSE POWER IS THE ONLY FORCE IN THE UNIVERSE THAT CAN SHATTER THE UNBREAKABLE GRIP OF A DEADLY TROLL!

SUDDENLY, THERE IS A BLINDING, SEARING, NERVE-SHATTERING BLAST, AND...

ODIN IS *FREE!* FOR WHEN HE PLUNGES HIS SWORD INTO THE GROUND, ANCHORING IT THERE, HE DRAWS UNTO HIMSELF THE LIMIT-LESS POWERS OF THE GODS!

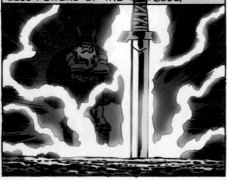

THEIR WILL TO FIGHT CRUMBLES BEFORE ODIN'S SHOW OF FORCE, AND THE TROLLS TELL HIM WHERE TO FIND *SURTUR!* SO, ODIN VENTURES FORTH ONCE MORE--INTO THE SEA OF FLAME!

SLOWLY, PONDEROUSLY, THE GIGANTIC HEAD OF EVIL *SURTUR*, KING OF THE FIRE DEMONS, RISES FROM BENEATH THE SWIRLING MASS OF MOLTEN LIQUID--AS ODIN FACES THE MONSTROUS CREATURE--UNAFRAID!

THEN, BEFORE THE VERY EYES OF THE RULER OF THE GODS, SURTUR'S LEFT HAND UNDER-GOES AN AWESOME CHANGE--AS HIS FINGERS ARE MAGICALLY TRANSFORMED INTO SINISTER SERPENTS!

BUT, BEFORE THE HUNGRY APPARITIONS CAN STRIKE, ODIN'S GREAT SWORD GESTURES SKYWARD--REACHING THROUGH THE EMPTINESS OF SPACE ITSELF...REACHING TO THE VERY END OF INFINITY!

AND, IN A SPLIT-SECOND, THE FROZEN REMNANTS OF LONG-DEAD PLANETS COME HURTLING DOWN TO SURTUR'S EVIL LAND OF FIRE!

3

AT THE MOMENT THEY ARE HIT WITH THE ICY SPACE WASTE, THE SERPENTS SHRIVEL UP AND BECOME HARMLESS, FOR FLAME CANNOT ENDURE SUCH BITTER COLD!

FOR LONG, SILENT MOMENTS, THE TWO MIGHTY ENEMIES FACE EACH OTHER, AS ODIN COMMANDS SURTUR TO OBEY HIS ROYAL COMMANDS--WHILE SURTUR KEEPS HIS DISTANCE, FEROCIOUSLY PLANNING HIS NEXT ATTACK!

AND THEN, SURTUR MAKES HIS MOVE! HE KNOWS HE CANNOT HARM ODIN HIMSELF, SO HE WILL STRIKE AT THE KING OF THE GODS BY DESTROYING THE ONE THING ODIN LOVES...THE PLANET *EARTH!*

SURTUR REACHES EARTH BEFORE ODIN CAN STOP HIM! EARTH, AROUND WHICH THE MAGIC TREE *YGGDRASILL* HAS SPREAD ITS BRANCHES, WHILE AWAITING THE COMING OF *MAN!*

BORING DEEP INTO THE CENTER OF THE PLANET, SURTUR RE-LEASES A HUGE CHUNK OF MATTER--A CHUNK WHICH FLIES INTO THE SKY WHERE IT WILL SPIN AROUND THE EARTH--AND BE FOREVER KNOWN AS-- THE *MOON!*

4

BUT, AT THE HOME OF THE GODS, *ODIN* FORMS THE SPARKLING *RAINBOW BRIDGE,* FOR THE FIRST TIME, TO SPEED HIS WAY TO EARTH!

THEN, AFTER REACHING HIS FAVORITE PLANET, ODIN HOLDS HIS GREAT SWORD ABOVE IT, DRAWING ON ALL THE ELECTRO-MAGNETIC PARTICLES OF THE COSMOS-- AND CONCENTRATING THEM ABOVE THE FERTILE PLANET...

SOON, THE POWERFUL FORCES CAUSE THE EARTH TO BEGIN *SPINNING,* FASTER AND FASTER AROUND THE SUN--AN ENDLESS ROTATION WHICH CONTINUES TO THIS VERY DAY...

AND WHICH TRAPS SURTUR IN THE CENTER OF THE PLANET, HOLDING HIM THERE BY CENTRIFUGAL FORCE-- KEEPING HIM AN ETERNAL PRISONER, WHERE HE FURNISHES HEAT AND ENERGY TO THE PLANET HE HAD HOPED TO DESTROY!

HOPING TO CAUSE ODIN TO SET HIM FREE, SURTUR SENDS A GIFT TO THE VICTORIOUS GOD... A GIFT WHICH FLIES THROUGH THE MOUTH OF A SPOUTING VOLCANO ...IT IS A WONDERFUL WINGED HORSE WHICH ODIN KEEPS--AS THE EVIL SURTUR HOPES THAT ONE DAY ODIN'S WRATH WILL BE APPEASED AND HE'LL BE FREED!

SURTUR CARES NOT *HOW* LONG IT TAKES... HE HAS ALL *ETERNITY* TO WAIT!

5

NEXT ISSUE: YOU'LL MARVEL AT-- THE *BOYHOOD OF THOR!*

THE END

STEALTHILY, SILENTLY, THOR STEALS INTO THE HUGE CASTLE OF THE TOWERING STORM GIANTS, FOLLOWED BY HIS RELUCTANT BROTHER!

MORE MEAT, MY FATHER! MY HUNGER IS RAVENOUS!

SUDDENLY, THE MALICIOUS *LOKI* MAKES A SURPRISE MOVE, PUSHING THE STARTLED THOR INTO FULL VIEW OF THE GIANTS!

IF YOU'RE SO ANXIOUS TO BE A *HERO*, THOR, I'LL GIVE YOU THE CHANCE! *THIS* IS THE TIME TO ATTACK -- WHILE THEIR THOUGHTS ARE ON THEIR FOOD!

YOU *FOOL!* THEY'LL *SEE* ME!

OR, PERHAPS LOKI IS *NOT* SUCH A FOOL! PERHAPS THAT WAS HIS *INTENTION!*

WHAT HAVE WE *HERE*??!

IT IS A PUNY ONE -- FROM THE LAND OF *ASGARD!* LET US *SLAY* HIM AS A WARNING TO OTHERS NOT TO ENTER OUR DOMAIN!

HOLD *YOUR TONGUE*, INSOLENT ONE! YOU SPEAK TO *THOR*, SON OF *ODIN!* I AM HERE TO RETURN THE GOLDEN APPLES TO IDUNA!

SO! *THAT* IS YOUR PURPOSE?!

HE WAS A FOOL TO *TELL* US!

DROWN THE YOUNG FOOL IN A TORRENT OF BROTH!

BUT, THOUGH YOUNG, *THOR* IS STILL A *GODLING* --WITH THE *STRENGTH* OF AN IMMORTAL!

GLUBBB!

IT IS *YOU* WHO SHALL PARTAKE OF THE BROTH-- NOT *ME!*

MOVING WITH BLINDING SPEED AND UNBELIEV-ABLE STRENGTH, THE YOUNG PRINCE HURLS A CRUDE *PEPPER* RECEPTACLE IN THE DIRECTION OF THE DAZED STORM GIANTS BEFORE THEY CAN MAKE A MOVE!

MY EYES.!! I CANNOT *SEE!*

THE TINY GODLING FIGHTS WITH THE FURY OF A CREATURE *POSSESSED!*

BUT THEN, A PRODIGIOUS SNEEZE, FROM LUNGS ENORMOUS ENOUGH TO TOPPLE A MOUNTAIN, BOWLS OVER THE HANDSOME YOUNG BATTLER!

3

AND, BEFORE THOR CAN REGAIN HIS BALANCE, HIS SWORD IS RENDERED USELESS BY A TITANIC FIST!

I'M *TRAPPED!*

HAH! SO *THIS* IS THE ONE WHO DARED DEFY US!

SEE HOW HELP-LESS HE IS NOW!

PERHAPS I SHALL *KEEP* HIM AND WEAR HIM TIED TO MY BELT AS AN ORNAMENT!

BUT, AT THAT MOMENT, THE WILY LOKI, WHO HAS NOT YET BEEN SEEN, TOSSES A PILE OF WET LEAVES INTO THE HUGE, FLAMING FIREPLACE...

AND, WITHIN SECONDS, THICK CLOUDS OF BLIND-ING SMOKE FILL THE VAST CHAMBER.

THERE MUST BE *ANOTHER* TINY ONE HIDDEN AMONG US!

WAIT NO LONGER! *KILL* HIM! SLAY THEM *ALL!*

BUT, UNDER COVER OF THE DENSE SMOKE, THE VALIANT THUNDER GOD STRIKES OUT AGAIN, WITH TELLING EFFECT!

AHH! I *KNEW* THIS WOULD MAKE YOU RELEASE YOUR HOLD ON ME!

THAT WAS QUICK THINKING, LOKI! NOW QUICKLY-- WE MUST FIND THE GOLDEN APPLES AND *FLEE!*

BAH! I DID NOT DO IT TO SAVE *YOU*-- MERELY TO CREATE A DIVERSION FOR *ME!* FOR I *KNOW* WHERE THE APPLES ARE HIDDEN!

4

THE END

AND, NO SOONER HAS LOKI RUN OFF THEN THE *EVIL ONES* ATTACK! *NEVER* HAS THERE BEEN SO AWESOME AN ARRAY OF IMMORTAL FOES...!!

the NORN HAG *riding* ULFRIN *the* DRAGON

the MERCILESS RIME GIANTS

I MUST PROTECT ASGARD --WITH MY *LIFE* IF NEED BE!

LAST of the ICE GIANTS

SKOLL & HATI, *the* WOLF GODS!

GEIRRODUR *the* TROLL

KNOWING HIS SWORD ALONE CANNOT HOLD BACK THE SURGING ATTACK OF THE EVIL ONES, THOR RESORTS TO CUNNING --TO TRICKERY-- AS HE CAUSES A GEYSER TO ERUPT WITH ONE BLOW OF HIS UNBREAKABLE BLADE!

I MUST DO WHAT I CAN TO GAIN TIME TILL HELP ARRIVES!

THESE MIGHTY ROCKS, STRUCK WITH ALL MY FORCE BY THE FLAT OF MY BLADE, WILL CAUSE SOME OF THE EVIL ONES TO DRAW BACK!! IF ONLY LOKI CAN BRING THE WARRIORS OF ASGARD IN TIME!

13

BUT, LITTLE DOES BRAVE THOR REALIZE, AS HE FACES THE ATTACK OF THE NORN HAG ON HER INCREDIBLE DRAGON, THAT LOKI HAS SUMMONED NO HELP!

WELL DONE, HAG! HE IS *TRAPPED!*

NOTHING THAT LIVES CAN WITHSTAND MY DRAGON'S ENCHANT- ED BREATH!

WEAKENED BY THE SMOKEY FUMES, HIS STRENGTH WANING--THOR SINKS TO HIS KNEES AS THE MIGHTY RIME GIANT WEAVES A SPELL ABOUT HIM...

AND, AT THE CONCLUSION OF THE SPELL, THE SON OF ODIN FINDS HIMSELF IN- EXORABLY TURNING INTO -- A *TREE!*

WHERE ARE THE WARRIORS?? IN ANOTHER FEW MINUTES, IT WILL BE TOO LATE FOR *ANYTHING* TO SAVE ME!!

BUT THEN, AS THOUGH IN ANSWER TO THOR'S IMPASSIONED PLEA, A MIGHTY WAR CRY IS HEARD...

FOR ODIN, AND ASGARD!!!

4

AS THE FIRST BLOW IS STRUCK, THE SPELL FALLS FROM YOUNG THOR, AND HE BECOMES THE IMMORTAL GODLING ONCE AGAIN!!

WE HEARD THE SOUNDS OF BATTLE, MY SON! IT WAS THE CLANGING OF YOUR SWORD THAT ALERTED US!

OH, BUT, FATHER, I HAVE FAILED! THE EVIL ONES WOULD HAVE DEFEATED ME IF NOT FOR YOUR ATTACK!

SPEAK NOT SO, YOUNG THOR! WITHOUT YOUR VALIANT DEFENSE, THEY WOULD HAVE BROKEN THROUGH THIS OPENING TO ASGARD! YOU HAVE GIVEN US THE TIME TO DEFEND OURSELVES! YOU HAVE SAVED ASGARD!

THEN, REALIZING THEY HAVE LOST THE ADVANTAGE OF SURPRISE... SEEING THE FURY WITH WHICH THE GODS OF ASGARD BATTLE -- THE EVIL ONES SLOWLY TURN AND STUMBLE BACK TO THE DARKNESS FROM WHENCE ___ THEY HAVE COME!

WHILE HE WHO WILL ONE DAY BE GOD OF THUNDER LIFTS THE URU HAMMER HIGHER THAN IT HAS EVER BEEN LIFTED BEFORE!!

I HAVE BEEN REWARDED WITH ADDITIONAL STRENGTH! SOON PERHAPS, SOON I SHALL BE ABLE TO LIFT THE MIGHTY HAMMER ABOVE MY HEAD! AND, ON THAT GLORIOUS DAY, IT WILL BE MINE TO CLAIM!

THAT DAY WILL NEVER COME, THOR! NOT SO LONG AS LOKI CAN LIFT A FINGER TO PREVENT IT!

THE END

MANY ARE THE SAGAS OF ASGARD, THE MYSTICAL LAND WHERE TITANS DWELL!! NEXT ISSUE WE BRING YOU ANOTHER IN THIS, THE MOST WIDELY-ACCLAIMED SERIES IN MODERN COMIC MAGAZINE HISTORY!

SEEING THOR, THE THREE FATES SENSE HIS REQUEST AND ANSWER HIM BEFORE HIS LIPS CAN FRAME THE QUESTION...

YOU **CAN** WIN ODIN'S ENCHANTED HAMMER-- BUT YOU WILL HAVE TO MEET **DEATH** FIRST!

THE FATES NEVER LIE! THIS MUST MEAN I'M **DOOMED!**

BUT I WILL NEVER STOP TRYING! I **MUST** HAVE THE MAGIC HAMMER!

AND IF I MUST **DIE** IN ORDER TO GET IT, THEN I SHALL FACE MY DESTINY WITH COURAGE-- AS THE SON OF ODIN **SHOULD!**

RETURNING TO ODIN'S PALACE, THE YOUNG GODLING ONCE MORE TRIES TO LIFT THE ALL-POWERFUL HAMMER-- BUT STILL CANNOT RAISE IT MORE THAN A FEW INCHES...

THIS IS THE HIGHEST I HAVE **EVER** RAISED IT-- BUT IT **STILL** IS NOT ENOUGH!

AT THAT MOMENT, BALDER, THE INNOCENT, STAGGERS INTO THE GREAT CHAMBER, COVERED WITH THE WOUNDS OF BATTLE...

THOR... THE STORM GIANTS-- AMBUSHED ME-- SEIZED MY SISTER-- SIF--

GENTLE SIF-- A PRISONER OF THE STORM GIANTS!! IT IS **UNTHINKABLE!**

2

HERE COME THE GUARDS TO ATTEND YOU, VALIANT BALDER! AS FOR ME, I SHALL RESCUE SIF FROM THE ENEMY, OR DIE TRYING! THIS I SWEAR TO YOU, MY FRIEND!!

THEN, FOR THE FIRST TIME IN HIS LIFE, THOR GRASPS THE MIGHTY HAMMER AND HOLDS IT HIGH OVER HIS HEAD!! BUT, SO INTENT UPON HIS MISSION IS HE THAT HE DOESN'T REALIZE WHAT HE IS DOING!

LET THE STORM GIANTS BEWARE!

LATER, AT THE OUTER APPROACHES TO THE CASTLE WHERE SIF IS IMPRISONED...

BEHOLD! IT IS THE PUNY GODLING! THIS TIME HE WILL NOT ELUDE US AGAIN!

TAKE CAUTION, BROTHER! THOUGH HIS SIZE IS SMALL COMPARED TO OURS, HE HAS THE STRENGTH AND VALOR OF MANY MEN!

I HAVE NO TIME TO WASTE WITH MERE CASTLE GUARDS! I MUST FIND THE LOVELY SIF, WITHIN THOSE WALLS!

THIS WILL ENABLE ME TO REACH THE CASTLE WITHOUT ANY FURTHER INTERFERENCE!

3

AND NOW TO RESCUE THE SISTER OF MY FRIEND BALDER!!

I KNOW THIS PLACE WELL! IT IS THE CASTLE OF KING RUGGA! THOUGH HE IS NOT A GOD HIMSELF, IT IS HIS DEAREST DESIRE TO *BECOME* ONE!

RUGGA, I HAVE COME FOR SIF!! FREE HER, OR SUFFER THE CONSEQUENCES!

WAIT, THUNDER GOD! LET ME *EXPLAIN!* HELA, THE GODDESS OF DEATH, HAS SWORN THAT SHE WOULD MAKE ME AN IMMORTAL IF I DELIVER SIF TO HER! SO-- I *DID!*

HEARTLESS ONE! YOU WOULD ACCEPT LIFE AT THE EXPENSE OF SOME-ONE ELSE'S DEATH?! TELL ME--WHERE CAN I *FIND* HELA! *SPEAK!*

DO NOT HARM ME! I SHALL TELL YOU WHERE TO FIND HER! BUT NO MAN IN HIS RIGHT MIND GOES TO FIND THE GODDESS OF DEATH!

4

BUT MIGHTY *THOR* IS *NOT* JUST A MERE MAN-- AND SO--

YOU *KNOW* THAT I AM *HELA*, GODDESS OF DEATH! AT MY TOUCH, EVEN A *GOD* MUST PERISH!

DO WITH ME WHAT YOU WILL-- BUT FREE THE INNOCENT SIF!

I OFFER *MYSELF* IN HER PLACE! LET *ME* FEEL YOUR FATAL TOUCH-- I KNOW NO FEAR!! BUT SET SIF FREE!

YOU WOULD SACRIFICE YOURSELF FOR ANOTHER? NEVER HAVE I HEARD SUCH AN OFFER!

I CANNOT DO IT! I CANNOT TAKE A LIFE WHICH IS SO YOUNG, SO BRAVE, SO NOBLE! GO, THOR, SON OF ODIN,... AND TAKE SIF WITH YOU! YOU HAVE EARNED HER FREEDOM!

AND SO IT WAS THAT THOR FIRST GAINED FULL POSSESSION OF HIS MAGIC HAMMER-- BY OFFERING TO MAKE THE SUPREME SACRIFICE-- GIVING UP HIS LIFE FOR THAT OF ANOTHER! AND THE IRONY OF THE TALE IS THIS-- NOT UNTIL *DAYS LATER* DID THE MIGHTY GOD REALIZE HE HAD WON HIS GOAL!

NEXT ISSUE: ANOTHER *TALE OF ASGARD*, FEATURING THE NOBLEST SUPER-HERO OF THEM ALL-- THE MIGHTY *THOR!!*

5

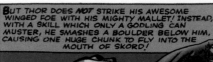

BUT THOR DOES *NOT* STRIKE HIS AWESOME WINGED FOE WITH HIS MIGHTY MALLET! INSTEAD, WITH A SKILL WHICH ONLY A GODLING CAN MUSTER, HE SMASHES A BOULDER BELOW HIM, CAUSING ONE HUGE CHUNK TO FLY INTO THE MOUTH OF SKORD!

THERE! BY THE TIME YOU HAVE DISLODGED THAT MAMMOTH ROCK, I SHALL BE SAFELY ON MY WAY!

NOW TO CONTINUE MY JOURNEY! ODIN WARNED ME IT WOULD BE FRAUGHT WITH PERIL, BUT I *MUST* SUCCEED! *WAIT--* I HEAR A VOICE--A THUNDEROUS, INHUMAN BELLOW--!

YOU SHALL GO NO FURTHER, PUNY GODLING --UNTIL YOU HAVE MET THE CHALLENGE OF *GULLIN,* MIGHTIEST OF THE BOAR GODS!

AND THOUGH *YOU* HAVE A HAMMER, *I* HAVE ONE, TOO! AND *MINE* IS FAR *BIGGER!*

AND THERE, ON THE OUTER FRINGES OF THE KINGDOM OF MIRMIR, ONE OF THE MOST TITANIC BATTLES OF ALL TIME TAKES PLACE, AS THE MIGHTY THOR AND THE GARGANTUAN GULLIN POUND AT EACH OTHER WITH PLANET-SHATTERING BLOWS-- NEITHER FOE MOVING BACK OR YIELDING A SINGLE INCH!

YOU HAVE COURAGE, THOR-- BUT IT IS USELESS AGAINST MY LARGER, MORE DEADLY HAMMER!

LARGER YOURS MAY BE, GULLIN-- BUT ONLY *MY* HAMMER WAS FORGED BY *ODIN* HIMSELF! *NOTHING* CAN WITHSTAND IT FOR LONG!

3

AND THE NEXT TREMENDOUS IMPACT DEMON-STRATES THE *TRUTH* OF MIGHTY THOR'S WORDS, AS GULLIN'S WEAPON IS SHATTERED TO BITS BEFORE HIS VERY EYES!

NOW YOU ARE *DEFENSELESS,* GULLIN! I ORDER YOU TO FLEE BEFORE MY HAMMER STRIKES AGAIN!

HE HAD NO CHOICE BUT TO ALLOW ME FREE PASSAGE! AND NOW, MY GOAL IS ALMOST AT HAND...

I MUST FOLLOW THIS MAIN STREAM WHICH WILL LEAD ME DIRECTLY TO KING MIRMIR HIMSELF!!

AND FINALLY, AT THE HEAD OF THE STREAM, BEHIND THE MYSTIC FOUNTAIN WHICH FEEDS ALL THE WORLD'S OCEANS, THOR FINDS THE ONE HE SEEKS!

THOR! IT IS *YOU!* DOES THAT MEAN MY MOMENT IS AT HAND?

YES! NOBLE ODIN HAS SENT YOU THIS MESSAGE --YOU MUST DO WHAT YOU ARE PLEDGED TO DO!

ODIN HAS SENT THIS BRANCH, FROM YGGDRASILL, THE TREE OF LIFE! YOU KNOW WHAT MUST BE DONE!

SO BE IT! MIRMIR WILL BE TRUE TO HIS SACRED TRUST! GIVE ME THE MAGIC BRANCH!

4

I PLACE THE BRANCH OF LIFE INTO THE ENCHANTED FOUNTAIN, AND SLOWLY STIR THE MYSTIC WATERS! NOW LET THEM SPILL INTO THE WORLD BELOW...

AND, FAR BELOW, IN THE PLACE CALLED *MIDGARD,* SOME OF THE MAGIC DROPS TRICKLE ONTO A PAIR OF TREES, AN ALDER AND AN ASH, PLANTED AGES BEFORE BY WISE ODIN...

...AND LO, THE TREES SLOWLY CHANGE FORM UNTIL... WHERE STOOD AN ALDER AND AN ASH, WE NOW SEE THE PROUD FIGURES OF *ASKE* AND *EMBLA,* DESTINED TO START A NEW RACE, IN THE IMAGE OF THE IMMORTALS OF ASGARD!

5

THUS, HIS MISSION ACCOMPLISHED, THE MIGHTY THOR RETURNS TO HIS HOME IN ASGARD, TO AWAIT THE NEWER AND MORE STARTLING TASKS WHICH ODIN HAS IN STORE!

THE END

EDITOR'S NOTE: FREELY TRANSLATED, THE TALE YOU HAVE JUST READ IS PART OF THE NORSE LEGENDS WHICH DEAL WITH THE BIRTH OF MANKIND AND THE DAYS BEFORE THE BEGINNING OF TIME!

NEXT ISSUE: THE START OF A NEW ASGARD SERIES! BIOGRAPHIES IN DEPTH OF THE DWELLERS OF ASGARD! OUR FIRST SUBJECT WILL BE *HEIMDALL,* GUARDIAN OF THE RAINBOW BRIDGE, AS ONLY STAN AND JACK CAN PRESENT HIM TO YOU!

AGES AGO THE RAINBOW BRIDGE SPANNED THE VAST DISTANCE FROM EARTH TO ASGARD WITH NONE TO GUARD IT! BUT THEN, ONE DAY, A VALIANT WARRIOR WAS SUMMONED TO THE THRONE ROOM OF MIGHTY ODIN...

YOU SENT FOR ME, MY LORD?

YES, LOYAL HEIMDALL! ASGARD HAS NEED OF YOUR COURAGE, YOUR FIDELITY, AND YOUR SKILL! HEAR THEN THE WORDS OF ODIN...

TOO LONG HAS THE RAINBOW BRIDGE REMAINED UNGUARDED! TOO MANY TIMES HAVE OUR ENEMIES ATTACKED ASGARD BY CROSSING ITS SHIMMERING SPAN! THE BRIDGE NEEDS A SENTRY!

LOOK, YOU! MARK HOW EVEN NOW A LABOR FORCE OF TROLLS WORKS TO REPAIR THE DAMAGE DONE TO THE WALLS OF ASGARD WHEN THE STORM GIANTS LAST CROSSED THE BRIDGE!

ONLY THOR'S MIGHTY HAMMER AND THE VALOR OF MY WARRIORS, SUCH AS YOU, SAVED ASGARD FROM BEING OVERRUN BY THE ENEMY!

AND THAT IS WHY I HAVE DECIDED TO APPOINT A GUARDIAN OF THE RAINBOW BRIDGE! I HAVE SELECTED THREE WARRIORS--AND NOW I SHALL CHOOSE ONE OF YOU!

2

AND SO... I WANT EACH OF YOU TO TELL ME WHY YOU THINK *YOU* SHOULD BE CHOSEN! *AGNAR THE FIERCE*, YOU SPEAK FIRST!

MY LUNGS ARE THE STRONGEST, LORD ODIN! *NONE* HAS A CHEST AS MIGHTY AS MINE!

BAH! OF WHAT IMPORTANCE IS *THAT?!!*

SILENCE, GOTRON!! YOUR TURN WILL COME NEXT!

NONE BUT *I* HAVE THE POWER TO BLOW A WARNING OF ATTACK ON THE ENCHANTED DRAGON HORN OF ASGARD--LIKE *THIS!!*

HE SPEAKS THE *TRUTH!* FOR AGES THE HORN HAS BEEN SILENT-- YET *NOW*, ITS ROAR REACHES TO THE VERY END OF INFINITY!!

AND WHAT OF YOU, *GOTRON, THE AGILE??*

MY DEEDS SPEAK FOR THEMSELVES, SIRE! SURELY YOU REMEMBER THAT I WAS NIMBLE ENOUGH TO DEFEAT *SEVEN* STORM GIANTS WHEN THEY ATTACKED ASGARD ONLY LAST YEAR!

THUS HAVE AGNAR AND GOTRON SPOKEN! AND NOW, *HEIMDALL THE FAITHFUL* MUST BE HEARD!

MY LORD ODIN, MY STRENGTH IS A MATCH FOR *ANY*-- BUT I HAVE *OTHER* ABILITIES --- I CAN SENSE APPROACHING DANGER BEFORE ANY OTHER! I SHALL *PROVE* IT IN YOUR GARDEN...

THEN, STEPPING OUT INTO THE LUSH GARDEN OF THE LORD OF ASGARD, HEIMDALL PUTS HIS EAR TO THE SOFT GRASS, AND SAYS,...

EVEN AT THIS MOMENT, I CAN HEAR THE TINIEST PLANT GROWING IN THE HEART OF THE HIDDEN HILLS!

YOU LIE! YOU SHALL FEEL THE BITE OF AGNAR'S *SWORD* FOR THIS!!

AND OF GOTRON'S *SPEAR!!*

3

STAND FAST!! ONLY ODIN COMMANDS HERE! WE SHALL SEE IF HEIMDALL LIES! GO, MY GARDENER...FLEE TO THE EXACT PLACE HEIMDALL MENTIONED AND SEE IF THERE GROWS A TINY PLANT!!

I OBEY, MY LORD! BUT IT CANNOT BE! NOTHING CAN GROW IN THE HIDDEN HILLS SINCE ONCE A DRAGON BREATHED HIS FIERY BREATH UPON THAT LAND!

EVEN NOW I HEAR THE TINY BUDS REACHING FOR THE SURFACE --EAGER TO FIND THE SUN!

TENSE MOMENTS LATER...

BY THE GODS!! HEIMDALL SPOKE THE TRUTH! AT THE VERY SPOT HE DESCRIBED-- A NEW PLANT--WHICH HAS JUST THIS SECOND BLOSSOMED INTO LIFE!!

THEN, WHEN THE ALMOST SPEECHLESS GARDENER RETURNS...

YOUR EARS INDEED ARE WONDROUS SHARP, LOYAL HEIMDALL! BUT I HAVE HEARD THAT YOU HAVE STILL OTHER POWERS!

THAT IS SO, MY LORD ODIN! NOTHING CAN ESCAPE THE SCANNING OF MY EYES!

I CAN LOOK ACROSS TIME, AS WELL AS SPACE !! EVEN NOW I SEE THE FAR-OFF APPROACH OF AN INVADING PARTY, MARCHING TOWARDS THE RAINBOW BRIDGE! THEY ARE A SAVAGE BAND OF STORM GIANTS, STILL A FULL TWO DAYS AWAY!

4

NOT DARING TO IGNORE HEIMDALL'S DRAMATIC WARNING, ODIN IMMEDIATELY DISPATCHES A HEAVILY-ARMED WAR PARTY TO MEET THE INVADERS BEFORE THEY CAN REACH THE VITAL RAINBOW BRIDGE!

CAN HEIMDALL *REALLY* HAVE SEEN AN ENEMY TWO DAYS AWAY??

THE WORDS OF LOYAL HEIMDALL ARE ALWAYS CLOAKED IN *TRUTH!*

AND, BEFORE THE WEEK HAS PASSED, THE WAR PARTY RETURNS--WITH A VALUABLE PRISONER --THE KING OF THE STORM GIANTS!

AGAIN YOUR WORDS HAVE BORNE THE RING OF TRUTH, HEIMDALL! YOUR WARNING HAS SAVED ASGARD FROM A DANGEROUS ATTACK!

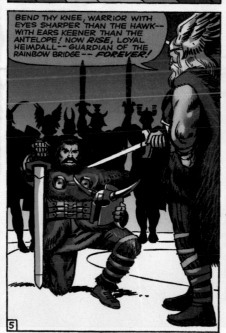

BEND THY KNEE, WARRIOR WITH EYES SHARPER THAN THE HAWK-- WITH EARS KEENER THAN THE ANTELOPE! NOW *RISE*, LOYAL HEIMDALL -- GUARDIAN OF THE RAINBOW BRIDGE -- *FOREVER!*

AND THUS STANDS HEIMDALL, THE ALL-SEEING, THE ALL-HEARING! HEIMDALL, THE EVER-VIGILANT! HEIMDALL, ETERNAL PROTECTOR OF THE FABLED LAND MEN CALL....*ASGARD!*

THAT'S ALL FOR NOW, TRUE BELIEVERS. BUT NEVER FEAR, A NEW THOR POCKETBOOK WILL BE COMING SOON!

5

ASGARD HOME OF THE NORSE GODS

NIFFLEHEIM

DOMAIN OF THE ICE GIANTS

ICE

HEL

VALHALLA

SEA OF MARMORA

TO SEA OF FEAR (UTGARD AND THRYHEIM)

ENCHANTED CHASM

ENCHANTED FOREST

PORTAL TO EARTH-DIMENSION

Sea of Space

GOPUL RIVER

KINGDOM OF THE DWARFS

FORE OF SIG

VALE OF CRYSTALS

CITY OF ASGARD

BIFROST

ASGARD

DOMAIN OF MOUNTAIN GIANTS

PLAIN OF IDA

ASGARD MOUNTAINS

TO LANDS OF MIMIR AND HYMIR

BOILING PLAIN

JOTUN

CAVERN OF TIME

KINGDOM OF RIVVAK (RAMPOK)

RUINS OF VANAHEIM

MUSPELHEIM

TEMPLE OF MYSTICS

TO GYMIRSGARD

100 MILES

KINGDOM OF HAROKIN

DOMAI OF ROCK TROLLS

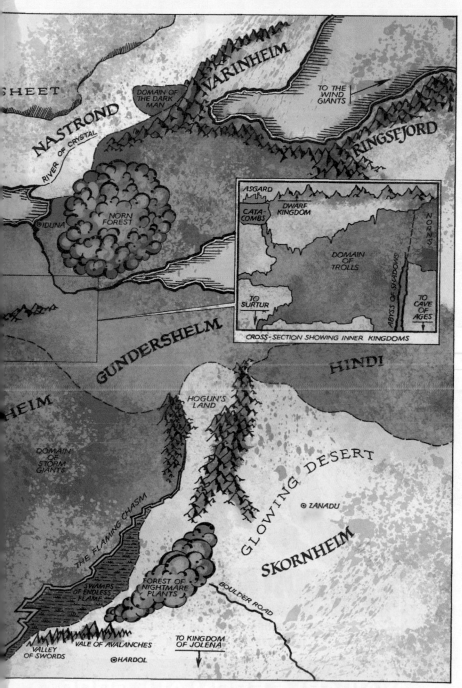

SHEET

NASTROND

VARINHEIM

DOMAIN OF THE DARK MAN

TO THE WIND GIANTS

RINGSFJORD

RIVER OF CRYSTAL

IDUNA

NORN FOREST

GUNDERSHELM

HINDI

...HEIM

HOGUN'S LAND

DOMAIN OF STORM GIANTS

GLOWING DESERT

ZANADU

SKORNHEIM

THE FLAMING CHASM

SWAMPS OF ENDLESS FLAME

FOREST OF NIGHTMARE PLANTS

BOULDER ROAD

VALLEY OF SWORDS

VALE OF AVALANCHES

TO KINGDOM OF JOLENA

HARDOL

ASGARD

DWARF KINGDOM

CATA-COMBS

NORNS

DOMAIN OF TROLLS

ABYSS OF SHADOWS

TO SURTUR

TO CAVE OF AGES

CROSS-SECTION SHOWING INNER KINGDOMS